MASS MURDER

A Brief History of Mass Murder in America

ISBN: 978-0-9993824-4-8

TABLE OF CONTENTS

INTRODUCTION
How Do We Define Mass Murder?

B efore we begin, let us take a moment to thank you for downloading *Mass Murder: A Brief History of Mass Murder in America*. We know there are many books on this topic available to you, and we truly appreciate that you have chosen ours. We are confident that you will find our book to be informative and educational, and we hope that if you enjoy the book, you will consider leaving us an honest review.

Mass murder has been a hot topic in the news lately - with school shootings and other tragedies dominating the headlines. Many people believe that the United States of America is becoming more violent, and that mass murder is becoming more prevalent. This book will examine the history of mass murder in America, the motives behind many of these tragedies, and what we can do to help prevent future tragedies.

Traditionally, mass murder has been defined as the murder of several people, in a short period of time, and within a close proximity to one another. This means that serial killers typically are not considered mass murderers, as they rarely kill more than one or two people at a time, and there often days or weeks between each killing spree. In January of 2013, the United States Congress officially defined mass murder as "a mass killing that results in at least three victims, excluding the perpetrator."

The term "mass murder" is usually used to describe a school shooting, a terrorist attack, or any other larger scale incident. Today, most mass murders involve firearms or homemade bombs, but throughout the history of mass murder, weapons of all kinds have been used - from firearms to knives to physical violence, and more.

Many studies now show that public shootings are becoming more common in the United States, meanwhile the overall rate of firearm deaths has actually decreased by 50% since 1993. From 1982 to 2011, a mass shooting occurred nearly every two hundred days. From 2011 to 2014, a mass shooting has occurred every 64 days in the United States. Not all of those incidents have been classified as "mass murders," however, as many of them had few (if any) fatalities.

So, why are mass murders happening more often?

Some people point to the rather relaxed gun control laws in the United States, insisting that if gun laws were stronger, there would be fewer mass shootings. Some people point to an increase in mental health issues, insisting that if mental health was a greater priority, we would be able to prevent mass murders from happening. Others point to the media, insisting that if the media handled news coverage of mass murders differently, there may be fewer of them. Many people believe that there is a "copycat effect" or that many mass murderers are seeking fame and attention - therefore, news coverage should be limited in order to avoid sensationalizing the act.

To really understand the root of the problem, we should review some of the most prominent mass murders in history. In the next chapter, we will discuss mass murders that occurred in the United States between 1800 and 1900. In following chapters, we will discuss mass murders from 1900 to 2000, and from 2000 to present day. Finally, we will discuss the various motives behind mass murders and what you can do to prevent these events. With a little bit of effort and a lot of understanding, we can all live in a healthier and safer world.

Always remember to take news coverage of mass murders with a large grain of salt. Media outlets tend to politicize and sensationalize these events. Many people assume that perpetrators of mass murders are usually foreigners or immigrants - in reality, they are usually white. Between 1982 and 2018, white perpetrators were responsible for 56 out of 97 mass shootings. 16 of those shootings had black perpetrators; there were seven each for Asians and Latinos, three for Native Americans, and the final eight were unknown or other.

In addition, many people tend to overlook the fact that mass murderers are predominantly male. Between 1982 and 2018, only 2 of 96 perpetrators were women. So, remember: these events are not always as they are portrayed. They are often politicized and sensationalized, with hundreds of conspiracy theories tacked onto them. Every story has two sides, and every action has a motive - unfortunately, some stories cannot be told and some motives cannot be discovered when the perpetrator has chosen to die.

TIMELINE

1856 - Pottowatomie Massacre

1857 - Dead Rabbits Riot

1863 - Hunstville, Alabama

1883 - Bisbee, Arizona

1888 - Hay Meadow Massacre

1894 - Rock Island Railroad

1910 - LA Times Bombing

1912 - Villisca, Iowa

1914 - Lexington Avenue Bombing

1922 - Perry Race Riot

1923 - Rosewood Massacre

1944 - Hartford Circus Fire

1958 - Starkweather Homicide

1964 - Pacific Airlines 773

1969 - Tate Murders

1973 - Upstairs Lounge

1974 - Gulliver's Nightclub

1974 - Ronald DeFeo, Jr. Murders

1975 - LaGuardia Airport Bombing

1977 - Golden Dragon Shooting

1978 - Blackfriars Massacre

1981 - Wonderland Murders

1984 - San Ysidro McDonald's Massacre

1986 - Edmond Post Office

1987 - Pacific Southwest Airlines 1771

1988 - Old Salisbury Road Massacre

1990 - Las Cruces Bowling Alley

1991 - Sacramento Hostage Crisis

1991 - University of Iowa

1992 - Lindhurst High School

1993 - 101 California Street Shooting

1993 - Aurora, Colorado

1993 - Long Island Railroad Shooting

1995 - Oklahoma City Bombing

1997 - Bellevue, Washington

1998 - Johnson & Golden Shooting

1999 - Columbine High School

1999 - Mark Barton Murders

1999 - Larry Ashbrook Murders

1999 - Xerox Murders

2000 - Wakefield Massacre

2001 - Isla Vista Murders

2001 - Nevada County Shootings

2001 - Greyhound Bus Attack]

2001 - Twin Towers

2003 - Lockhead Martin Shooting

2004 - Deltona Massacre

2005 - Red Lake Indian Reservation

2005 - Glendale Train Crash

2006 - Goleta Post Office

2006 - Amish School Shooting

2007 - Trolley Square Shooting

2007 - Virginia Tech School Shooting

2007 - Westroads Mall Shooting

2008 - Northern Illinois Univ. Shooting

2009 - Farmville Murders

2009 - Carthage Nursing Home

2009 - American Civic Assoc. Shooting

2009 - Fort Hood Shootings

2010 - University of Alabama Shooting

2010 - Hartford Distributors Shooting

2011 - Seal Beach Shooting

2011 - Maksim Gelman Murders

2011 - Tucson Shootings

2012 - Century 16 Theater Shooting

2012 - Wisconsin Sikh Temple Shooting

2012 - Sandy Hook Elementary School

2013 - Navy Yard Shooting

2013 - Santa Monica Shooting

2013 - West Fertilizer Co. Explosion

2014 - Isla Vista Stabbing/Shooting

2014 - Fort Hood Shooting

2015 - Charleston Church Massacre

2015 - Chattanooga Shooting

2015 - Umpqua Community College

2015 - Planned Parenthood Shooting

2015 - Inland Regional Center Shooting

2016 - Pulse Nightclub Shooting

2017 - First Baptist Church Shooting

2017 - Las Vegas Massacre

2018 - Stoneman Douglas High School

CHAPTER 1
Mass Murders, 1800 to 1950

W e begin by talking about mass murders in the 1800s simply because any mass murders that occurred before 1800 are poorly documented. There is little proof and much conjecture regarding those events. Mass murders that occurred in the 1800s and later were well-documented in newspapers, and we therefore have a lot more information about them.

TIMELINE

1856 - Pottowatomie Massacre
1857 - Dead Rabbits Riot
1863 - Hunstville, Alabama
1883 - Bisbee, Arizona
1888 - Hay Meadow Massacre
1894 - Rock Island Railroad
1910 - LA Times Bombing
1912 - Villisca, Iowa
1914 - Lexington Avenue Bombing
1922 - Perry Race Riot
1923 - Rosewood Massacre
1944 - Hartford Circus Fire

1856 - Pottawatomie Massacre

Prior to the American Civil War, the city of Lawrence, Kansas was sacked by pro-slavery groups. There were no deaths resulting from the sacking, but a lot of damage was done to shops and other local businesses in Lawrence. In retaliation for the sacking, an abolitionist group attacked a settlement in Franklin County, Kansas, near Pottawatomie Creek. The attack occurred overnight, from May 24th to May 25th, and five pro-slavery settlers were killed as a result. This was considered one of the most violent acts prior to the start of the Civil War.

1857 - Dead Rabbits Riot

On July 4th and 5th, two gangs in New York City began protesting local police administration. The Dead Rabbits gang and the Bowery Boys gang were traditionally enemies, and the protest quickly turned into a full-blown riot - with the two gangs fighting with one another. This is considered one of the biggest and most violent gang riots in history - with eight deaths and approximately a hundred injuries. There may have been many more deaths and injuries than reported, as most of the gang members feared retaliation and refused to seek medical treatment. A number of movies have been made about this event, with the most prominent being *Gangs of New York*.

1863 - Huntsville, Alabama

On January 10th, in the midst of the American Civil War, Union soldiers executed nine men - three of which were Confederate soldiers. The nine men had been captured and held as prisoners, as they were suspected of being Confederate sympathizers that assisted in a guerilla-style attack on twenty-five Union soldiers a month before. Formal charges were never filed against the Union soldiers involved, but the commanding officer was discharged.

1883 - Bisbee, Arizona

On December 8th, five outlaw cowboys robbed a general store in Bisbee and killed four people inside the store. Four of the five men wore masks, but the fifth did not - and he was quickly identified by locals. Over the next few weeks, the other outlaws were also identified - along with a sixth person that was considered to be the "ringleader." The ring leader, John Heath, was sentenced to life in prison. This sentence was not accepted by Bisbee locals, and a lynch mob formed. The lynch mob broke into the prison, forcibly removed Heath, and he was hanged on February 22nd, 1884. The other five outlaws were publicly hanged in March of 1884 - these were the first public hangings in the history of Bisbee, and the bodies were buried in what is now a famous "Old West" cemetery. Their graves can still be visited in Bisbee today.

1888 - Hay Meadow, Kansas

In 1888, Stevens County, Kansas, had no official county seat. Two different towns were vying for the honor - Hugoton and Woodsdale. On July 25th, 1888, a group of men that supported the Hugoton claim planned a recreational outing in area south of the county line called No Man's Land. On their way there, they were ambushed by a group of Woodsdale supporters, including the marshal of Woodsdale. Reinforcements were called in, and when all was said and done, the Woodsdale group was captured, disarmed and executed. The Hugoton group was eventually convicted, and seven men were sentenced to death - but those convictions were overturned when the Supreme Court ruled that the court that handed down those prosecutions (Paris, Texas) had no jurisdiction.

1894 - Rock Island Railroad - Lincoln, Nebraska

On August 9th, a railroad train carrying two passenger cars and thirty-three passengers was deliberately derailed. As the train passed over a trestle bridge above the Salt Creek, the trestle began to separate and collapse, and the train fell into the Salt Creek. When the train crashed, the engine exploded - setting both the train and the trestle bridge on fire. Eleven passengers, mostly from the first passenger car, were killed. Twenty-two were saved. The fire on the trestle bridge could not be put out, so they allowed it to burn. Only after the fire died out could they begin their investigation - where it was found that railroad spikes had been pulled and railroad ties had been pulled apart with a crowbar. Eventually, an African American man was arrested, and tried twice for sabotage, but a verdict could not be reached. This case remains unsolved.

1910 - LA Times Bombing - Los Angeles, California

On October 1st, a member of the International Association of Bridge and Structural Iron Workers union planted a dynamite bomb in the alleyway beside the Los Angeles Times building. The dynamite was connected to a clock, which as used as a detonator. The dynamite exploded around one o'clock in the morning, collapsed part of the three-story building, and ignited a natural gas pipeline. The fire from the natural gas pipeline destroyed not only the Los Angeles Times building, but the printing press, as well. At the time of the bombing, 115 staffers were inside the building, preparing a special edition of the newspaper. Of those 115 staffers, twenty-one of them died - two from the initial explosion and nineteen from the subsequent fire.

The bombing was part of a labor strike organized by the union and was meant to draw attention to their cause. A number of prior bombings had occurred in the years before, but none of those bombings led to any fatalities - just damaged property. The union was quick to condemn the LA Times bombing, even as more bombs were found at the home of the newspaper's publisher and owner.

After weeks of fruitless investigation by the Los Angeles Police Department, the Los Angeles mayor, George Alexander, hired a private detective to find the perpetrators. During his undercover investigation, the private eye was eventually able to obtain a confession from a union organizer named J.B. McNamara. McNamara's associate, Ortie McManigal, was also arrested. The two were extradited to California, and a third arrest was made - that of McNamara's brother, J.J. McNamara.

The McNamara brothers eventually took a plea deal - J.B. was sentenced to life in prison, and J.J. was given a much shorter prison term. The brothers insisted that they had no idea the building was staffed, and that they had only intended to cause damage to the building - they did not intend to kill anyone. After their trial, a number of other union members were brought up on charges by the federal government, leading to the collapse of the labor movement in Los Angeles.

1912 - Villisca, Iowa

On the evening of June 9th, eight people were murdered in a home in Villisca, Iowa. Each of the eight victims was found to have severe head wounds, from being bludgeoned with an axe. The victims included Josiah Moore, his wife Sarah, their four children (Herman, Mary Catherine, Arthur and Paul), as well as two other children that were friends of the family (Ina Mae and Lena Stillinger). The family was last seen alive around 10 P.M. that evening, leaving church. Their bodies were found by a neighbor at 7 A.M. the next morning.

It was suspected that the murdered hid in the attic and waited for the family to return from church, killing them sometime between midnight and 5 A.M. The parents were killed first, then the children. Investigators believed that all but one of the victims were asleep when they were killed. The last victim, a young girl named Lena, was not only awake during the attack - but may have also been sexually assaulted.

Little evidence was found in the house, but Reverend George Kelly was eventually arrested and tried twice. The first trial ended with a hung jury and the second trial ended with an acquittal. Kelly was a traveling minister, with a history of mental instability and several accusations of inappropriate behavior towards young women and girls.

A number of other suspects were considered, but without evidence, no one else was arrested and the case remains unsolved.

1914 - Lexington Avenue, New York City

On July 4th, there was an explosion in an apartment on Lexington Avenue, killing four people and injuring many others. The explosion was caused by a bomb that had detonated prematurely - a bomb that had been meant to blow up the home of John D. Rockefeller. Three of the four people who died were part of the plot to bomb Rockefeller's home. This is considered one of the first acts of terrorism to be documented in the United States.

1922 - Perry Race Riot - Perry, Florida

On December 14th, an African American man was lynched and burned at the stake, after a white schoolteacher was murdered. Charles Wright, the African American that was killed, was an escaped convict that had been arrested for the murder of the schoolteacher. While in jail, a mob of several thousand community members forcibly removed him from the jail, forced him to confess to the murder, and then burned him alive.

During the riot, two other African Americans were shot and hanged, and a number of buildings were burned (including the only African American school in town, a Masonic lodge, a church and several homes).

1923 - Rosewood Massacre - Levy County, Florida

During the first week of January, a race riot destroyed the town of Rosewood, Florida. Officially, six African Americans and two white people were killed, but many eyewitnesses claim that as many as 150 people were killed during the riot. Nearly every structure and building was burned during the riot. Residents that were able to escape hid in nearby swamps until they could be evacuated. After the riot, the town was abandoned - no one ever returned, no one was ever arrested or charged, and very few official records or documents regarding the riot actually exist. By the time an official investigation was conducted, many of the eyewitnesses had died of unrelated causes/issues, and there was little reliable information available. The official death toll remains at eight - but many, many witnesses claim up to 150 were killed (both African American and white), and that the bodies were buried in a mass grave in Levy County.

1944 - Hartford Circus Fire - Connecticut

On July 6th, during a Ringling Brothers and Barnum & Bailey performance, a fire started on the southwest wall of the tent. Because the tent was treated with paraffin wax to make it waterproof, the fire spread very quickly with nearly 7,000 people in attendance (mostly women and children), panic quickly ensued. Approximately 168 people were killed, with more than 700 treated for injuries. The vast majority of deaths and injuries were the result of the fire itself, but there were a number of deaths and injuries that resulted from the stampede as people tried to escape. No circus animals were harmed during the fire.

It is believed that the fire was the result of an arsonist, Robert Segee. At the time of the fire, Segee would have been only fourteen-years-old. At the time of his confession in 1950, he claimed to work for the circus as a "roustabout" or assistant. Segee was eventually arrested and sentenced to forty-four years in prison for unrelated arson charges. He was never officially charged with or convicted for the circus fire, as his history of mental illness would have made him difficult to prosecute without physical evidence, which did not exist. Officially, the fire remains unsolved.

Summary

You may note that the majority of the mass murders that occurred between 1800 and 1950 were the result of racial tensions and political uprisings. As you read through the next chapter, Mass Murders from 1950-2000, you will notice a distinct shift in motivations. Many of the mass murders will be more targeted, more personal.

CHAPTER 2
1950 - 2000

We will now detail a series of mass murders that occurred between 1950 and 2000 in the United States of America. Many of these murders were high profile, and it is likely that you have heard the stories before - for example, you have probably heard of Charles Manson and the murder of Sharon Tate, the Wonderland murders, the Oklahoma City Bombing, and the Columbine High School shooting. We will discuss each of these events and more.

TIMELINE

1958 - Starkweather Homicide
1964 - Pacific Airlines 773
1969 - Tate Murders
1973 - Upstairs Lounge
1974 - Gulliver's Nightclub
1974 - Ronald DeFeo, Jr. Murders
1975 - LaGuardia Airport Bombing
1977 - Golden Dragon Shooting
1978 - Blackfriars Massacre
1981 - Wonderland Murders
1984 - San Ysidro McDonald's Massacre
1986 - Edmond Post Office

1987 - Pacific Southwest Airlines 1771
1988 - Old Salisbury Road Massacre
1990 - Las Cruces Bowling Alley
1991 - Sacramento Hostage Crisis
1991 - University of Iowa
1992 - Lindhurst High School
1993 - 101 California Street Shooting
1993 - Aurora, Colorado
1993 - Long Island Railroad Shooting
1995 - Oklahoma City Bombing
1997 - Bellevue, Washington
1998 - Johnson & Golden Shooting
1999 - Columbine High School
1999 - Mark Barton Murders
1999 - Larry Ashbrook Murders
1999 - Xerox Murders

1958 - Starkweather Homicide - Nebraska

In January of 1958, Charles Starkweather killed ten people over a span of eight or nine days. He began his killing spree on January 21st by murdering the parents of his teenage girlfriend (Caril Fugate), along with her two-year-old sister. He hid their bodies in the house and waited for his girlfriend to return home. When she finally arrived, he told her that her family was being held hostage and they would only be safe if she cooperated and did exactly as he told her to. The two remained barricaded in the house until January

27th, when police were finally alerted that the parents had not been seen in approximately a week.

Starkweather took Fugate to a friend's home nearby. Upon arrival, he killed the family friend, along with the friend's dog. They continued to flee police pursuit, and eventually ran their car off the road. Two local teenagers offered to help, thinking they were stranded, and Starkweather forced the teens to drive them to an abandoned storm cellar. After arriving at the storm cellar, Starkweather shot and killed one of the teens, then attempted to rape the other. When he was unable to do so, he shot and killed her, then fled with Fugate in the teens' car.

Starkweather drove himself and Fugate to Nebraska, where he forced his way into a home in a wealthy neighborhood. Starkweather murdered the wife of the household, along with a maid, and then snapped the neck of the family dog. He and Fugate then hid in the household, waiting for the husband to return home. When he did, Starkweather shot and killed him, then stole a collection of jewelry, as well as their car, and they fled.

While on the run, they found a traveling salesman, asleep in his car on the side of the road. Knowing he needed a different vehicle to avoid law enforcement, he shot and killed the salesman and attempted to steal the vehicle. Unfamiliar with parking brakes, he had difficulty driving away and the car stalled out. A good Samaritan stopped to help him with the vehicle, and

Starkweather threatened him with a gun. They began to fight, and as they fought, a Deputy Sheriff arrived at the scene.

Upon seeing the Sheriff, Starkweather's girlfriend, Fugate, ran to the sheriff and identified Starkweather immediately. Starkweather managed to get the car started and led police on a high-speed chase. Only after police shot out his windshield did Starkweather stop the car and surrender.

Starkweather claimed repeatedly that Fugate had assisted him in the assaults and murders, but Fugate maintained her innocence throughout the investigation. Starkweather was eventually convicted and sentenced to death. He was executed in June of 1959.

1964 - Pacific Airlines 773 - California

In May, an airliner crashed in California as the result of a mass murder-suicide. Francisco Gonzalez shot both the pilot and co-pilot, just minutes before the plane was scheduled to land. He then shot himself. As a result, the plane crashed, and all forty-four passengers were killed. The plane crashed into a hillside and exploded on impact - those that were not killed as a result of the impact were likely killed in the explosion or subsequent fire.

During the investigation, detectives found that Gonzalez was deep in debt, had gambled a large amount of money in Reno, Nevada the night before the flight, and had taken out a last-minute life insurance policy with his wife listed as the beneficiary.

1969 - Tate Murders - Los Angeles, California

Over a two-day span in August, members of the Manson Family cult murdered five people in a Hollywood home - including actress Sharon Tate, who was eight months pregnant. In addition to Tate, they murdered three friends of Tate's, along with a teenage visitor as he tried to leave. Some of the victims were shot and some were stabbed. The pregnant Tate was stabbed no less than sixteen times, despite her pregnancy and pleas for her life. The Tate murders were highly publicized, and more information about the murders, and the Manson Family, can be found in the book *Helter Skelter* by Vincent Bugliosi and Curt Gentry.

1973 - Upstairs Lounge - New Orleans, Louisiana

On June 24th, a fire was set in a gay bar, located on the second floor of a building in New Orleans' French Quarter. It is believed that the fire was started on the first-floor staircase by a bar patron that had been kicked out of the bar earlier that night - but no charges were ever filed, and the case officially remains unsolved. Twenty-eight people died in the fire, one died on the way to the hospital, three died in the hospital, and fifteen others suffered serious injuries. The man believed to be responsible for the fire died by suicide in 1974.

1974 - Gulliver's Nightclub - Greenwich, Connecticut

On June 30th, a bowling alley on the border of Greenwich, Connecticut and Port Chester was burglarized and then set on fire. The fire quickly spread to a nightclub next door, where twenty-four people died, and thirty-two people were injured (thirteen of which were firefighters). Most of the deaths were the result of smoke inhalation, as people were trapped on the dance floor. Peter Leonard was eventually arrested for the crime. After pleading guilty, he was sentenced to fifteen years in prison.

1974 - Ronald DeFeo, Jr. - Amityville

On November 13th, Ronald DeFeo, Jr., murdered his six members of his family - his parents, two sisters and two brothers. Each one was shot in their bed, and investigators reported that each person was asleep when they were shot. DeFeo first claimed that his family had been killed by a mob hit man, but after discovering multiple inconsistencies in his story, detectives obtained a confession from DeFeo. In 1975, DeFeo was found guilty on all six counts and sentenced to 25 years to life in prison. This story has been retold many times, and you may recognize it as the film *Amityville Horror*.

1975 - LaGuardia Airport - New York City, New York

On December 9th, a bomb was set off near the baggage claim at the LaGuardia airport in New York City. Eleven people were killed, and seventy-four people were injured in the blast. To this day, this bombing remains unsolved, although it is believed to have been a terrorist action by Croatian nationals.

1977 - Golden Dragon - San Francisco, California

On September 4th, a gang-related shooting in a San Francisco restaurant killed five people and injured eleven people. None of the victims were actually members of the gangs involved in the shooting. The Mayor of San Francisco offered a $25,000 reward for information, which was later raised to a $100,000 reward by the end of September. In response to the large reward, a gang member came forward and provided police with a recorded confession by another gang member. Ultimately, five gang members were arrested and convicted.

1978 - Blackfriars Massacre - Boston, Massachusetts

On June 28th, five people were killed in downtown Boston bar called Blackfriars, as a result of tensions between the Irish mob and the Italian-American mafia. It is believed that the victims were killed because of a dispute over a cocaine sale, but little is actually known about the incident. Two suspects were tried and acquitted, and the incident remains unsolved today.

1981 - Wonderland Murders - Los Angeles, California

On July 1st, five people were attacked in a home in Laurel Canyon, California. Four of the victims were bludgeoned to death with hammers and metal pipes, and the fifth was also badly beaten - but alive. The fifth victim survived the attack but was left with permanent amnesia. The motive for the murders was retaliation for a violent robbery committed by the victims in the days before, and ultimately the incident has been ruled one of "gang violence." Over the years, several members of a rival gang have been tried, but all have been acquitted for lack of evidence and the case remains officially unsolved.

1984 - San Ysidro McDonald's Massacre - San Ysidro, California

On July 18th, James Huberty entered a McDonald's restaurant and opened fire. Seventeen people were killed inside the restaurant, including three children. Four were killed in the restaurant parking lot, including two children. Nineteen were injured, including eight children. Police responded to the incident within ten minutes, and Huberty was ultimately shot and killed by a SWAT Sniper. His motive for the attack remains unclear, but his wife told investigators that he had lost his job the week before, and that he had been concerned for his mental health and had actually reached out to a mental health clinic several days before the shooting. When the mental health clinic failed to return his call, he told his wife that his "life was over."

1986 - Edmond Post Office - Edmond, Oklahoma

On August 20th, a disgruntled postal worker attacked his co-workers - shooting twenty and killing fourteen of them. Patrick Sherrill then killed himself before police could arrive. It is believed that Sherrill's motive was related to his poor job performance and conflicts with management. As a result of this massacre, and seven other postal office shootings that have occurred since, the phrase "going postal," has become very popular.

1987 - Pacific Southwest Airlines 1771

On December 7th, David Burke shot and killed the pilot and copilot of Pacific Southwest Airlines, Flight 1771. He then forced the plane into a nosedive, and the airplane crashed into a hillside - traveling at such a high speed that it disintegrated on impact. All forty-three passengers and crew members died. Burke was a former employee of USAir who had been fired in the days before the attack for petty theft.

1988 - Old Salisbury Road Massacre - South Carolina

On July 17th, Michael Hayes stood on the centerline of Old Salisbury Road and shot nine different people driving along the road. Of those nine, four died. Hayes worked in a moped shop on Old Salisbury Road, and later claimed that he thought those driving by were demons that needed to be killed. He pleaded not guilty by reason of insanity, and a jury agreed. In lieu of a prison sentence, he was committed to a mental hospital in Raleigh, for treatment of schizophrenia, alcohol dependence, and a personality disorder. In 2012, Hayes was released.

1990 - Las Cruces Bowling Alley Massacre - New Mexico

On February 10th, two people robbed the Las Cruces Bowl bowling alley, shot seven people (killing four), and then set fire to the building. One victim managed to call for emergency services, despite having been shot five times himself, and saved the lives of the other three victims. Today, the case remains unsolved - with no suspects ever being arrested or tried.

1991 - Sacramento Hostage Crisis - California

On April 4th, four gunmen attempted to rob a Good Guys! electronics store. When the robbery went awry, the gunmen took forty-one people hostage. Three hostages were subsequently killed, as well as three of the four gunmen. Fourteen hostages were injured, and the one remaining gunman was taken into custody by police. That gunman, Loi Khac Nguyen, was sentenced to forty-one consecutive life terms in prison.

1991 - University of Iowa - Iowa City, Iowa

On November 1st, Gang Lu shot and killed four faculty members and one student, while leaving another student seriously injured, during an altercation on the University of Iowa campus. Lu was a former graduate student that was unhappy about not winning a prize for his graduate dissertation. While attending a meeting for a theoretical space plasma physics research group, he opened fire on attendees, then fled to another room and killed himself.

1992 - Lindhurst High School - Olivehurst, California

On May 1st, a former student opened fire at Lindhurst High School. Three students and one teacher were killed, and nine other students and one teacher were wounded. The former student, Eric Houston, then surrendered himself to police custody. During the investigation, Houston told detectives that he had been upset about losing his job and was worried he would unable to obtain another job, as he had failed to complete high school and had neither a high school diploma or a GED. Houston was sentenced to death and is currently on death row in a California prison.

1993 - 101 California Street Shooting - San Francisco, California

On July 1st, Gian Ferri entered a law firm office and opened fire. Eight people were killed, and six were injured. Ferri killed himself before police could apprehend him. His motive for the shooting is still unknown, despite a note he left behind. Although the letter was typed, the grammar and misspellings were so severe that the letter was almost entirely unintelligible. What little could be discerned from the letter implied that Ferri believed he had been poisoned with MSG and outlined a long list of complaints against the Food and Drug Administration, the legal profession as a whole, and several particular law firms. During the investigation, detectives found that this particular law firm had never actually assisted Ferri with anything legal and had only ever referred him to a different law firm for an out-of-state matter.

1993 - Aurora, Colorado

On December 14th, Nathan Dunlap opened fire in a Chuck E. Cheese restaurant - killing four employees and injuring a fifth. Dunlap was a former employee of the business and had been fired several months prior to the shooting. Dunlap fled the scene after stealing money from the register. He was apprehended, found guilty, and sentenced to death. In 2013, while on death row, Dunlap received a temporary stay of execution from Colorado Governor John Hickenlooper, and as long as Hickenlooper remains governor, he will not be executed.

1993 - Long Island Rail Road Shooting - Garden City, New York

On December 7th, Colin Ferguson boarded the Long Island Rail Road train and opened fire on passengers. Six people were killed and nineteen were injured before Ferguson was stopped by three other passengers (Kevin Blume, Mark McEntee, and Mike O'Connor). Passengers restrained Ferguson until an off-duty police officer boarded the train and took him into custody. Investigators found several pieces of paper in Ferguson's pockets that detailed apparent reasons for the attack - many of which referred to racism. Ferguson was sentenced to 315 years and eight months in prison.

1995 - Oklahoma City Bombing - Oklahoma

On April 19th, a truck bomb went off in the Alfred P. Murrah Federal Building, killing 168 people and injuring 680 others. The explosion destroyed one-third of the building and caused damage to over three hundred buildings in the surrounding neighborhood. Total cost of damage was estimated at $652 million. Timothy McVeigh was arrested less than two hours after explosion, on his way outside of Oklahoma. His original arrest was for weapons found during a traffic stop. McVeigh was ultimately found guilty and executed in 2001. His partner in the crime, Terry Nichols, was tried twice and eventually sentenced to 161 consecutive life sentences.

1997 - Bellevue, Washington
On January 3rd, two teenagers lured an older girl to a park and murdered her, then broke into her family home and murdered her parents and her sister. Each teen, Alex Baranyi and David Anderson, were sentenced four consecutive life sentences. The motives behind their attack were never made clear, and both teens tried to explain it away as "just something they wanted to experience."

1998 - Mitchell Johnson & Andrew Golden - Jonesboro, Arkansas
On March 24th, Mitchell Johnson and Andrew Golden shot and killed four students and a teacher, and wounded ten others, during an incident at the Westside Middle School in Craighead County, Arkansas. Johnson, age 13, and Golden, age 11, were students at the school. Both students had reputations for causing trouble and starting fights. On the day of

the shooting, they stashed a number of guns and a lot of ammunition in the woods behind the school, then pulled the firearm. As the students and teachers evacuated the building, the boys opened fire. They then tried to flee to a van they had loaded with camping supplies and survivalist gear but were caught. Both boys claimed they hadn't meant to kill anyone and that they "just wanted to scare them." Each boy was sentenced to confinement (juvenile detention) until they reached the age of 21, upon which they then had to be released, according to the maximum sentencing guideline in Arkansas at the time. Johnson was released in 2005, and Golden was released in 2007. Since their original release, Johnson has since been re-incarcerated and released on other, unrelated charges. Little is known about Grant and his whereabouts.

1999 - Columbine High School

On April 20th, two high school students fatally shot twelve students and one teacher, injured twenty-four others, and then killed themselves. Eric Harris and Dylan Klebold planted fire bombs, propane tank bombs, car bombs, and 99 other explosive devices throughout the school. They also had a wealth of guns and ammunition available to them at the time of the attack.

According to personal journals found after the attack, Harris and Klebold had planned a large-scale bombing - meant to resemble the Oklahoma City

Bombing. When the bombs failed to go off, they relied entirely on their guns, Molotov cocktails, and a few small pipe bombs. They wandered throughout the school, killing indiscriminately. Approximately an hour after the incident, both Harris and Klebold took their own lives. Reports indicated that they may have killed themselves simultaneously, as a suicide pact.

The ultimatum conclusion made by investigators was that Harris was a clinical psychopath with a messianic-level superiority complex, while Klebold was depressive. The assumption has been that while Dylan simply wanted to die, Klebold wanted to kill as many as he could. They spent nearly a year planning the attack together, gathering supplies, and building bombs.

In the aftermath, many people blamed bullying for the actions of Harris and Klebold, along with goth subculture and violent video games. Others blamed "dark music," like heavy metal, and cult films like *Natural Born Killers*. Ultimately, everyone can likely agree that Harris and Klebold's actions were the result of mental illness.

1999 - Mark O. Barton - Atlanta, Georgia

On July 29th, Mark Barton killed twelve people and injured thirteen others in Stockbridge, Georgia, outside of Atlanta. The attacks began in the early morning of July 27th, when Barton bludgeoned his wife to death while she slept. The next night, on July

28th, he beat both of his children to death, as well. Then, on July 29th, he entered the offices of his former employer and opened fire. He shot five people in the office, four of whom died, and then entered a nearby business and killed another five people. Four hours after the attack, Barton attempted to take a hostage but was unsuccessful. Before he could be apprehended by law enforcement, he committed suicide. A total of twelve people were killed, not including Barton. Notes were found in Barton's home that led investigators to assume his motives were related to the loss of a substantial amount of money, along with severe depression. Barton had previously been suspected in the deaths of his first wife and her mother, as well.

1999 - Larry Ashbrook - Fort Worth, TX

On September 15th, Larry Ashbrook shot and killed seven people, injured seven more, and then committed suicide. Ashbrook interrupted a prayer rally at the Wedgewood Baptist Church. Of the seven people killed, four of them were teenagers. Ashbrook argued with another member of the prayer group and then killed himself. Several remarks made by Ashbrook during the altercation implied that Ashbrook's motive stemmed from a distaste for the Baptist religion. Ashbrook had also displayed paranoia, as well as aggressive tendencies, in the days leading up to the event.

1999 - Xerox Murders - Honolulu, Hawaii

On November 2nd, Bryan Uyesugi shot and killed seven people (all co-workers) at the Xerox Corporation building in Honolulu. After the shooting, Uyesugi stole a company vehicle and fled the scene. He was found in downtown Honolulu, where he threatened to shoot children inside the Nature Center building where he was parked off. A police standoff lasted for nearly five hours before he was finally apprehended. Uyesugi had been reprimanded at work in the weeks prior to the incident for refusing to train on a new piece of equipment. He told investigators that he wanted to "give them a reason" to fire him, with the reason being the shooting. Uyesugi ultimately pleaded not guilty by reason of insanity, but that defense was rejected. He was sentenced to life in prison without the possibility of parole, and he was fined $70,500 dollars. As Hawaii does not have the death penalty, his sentence was adjusted to a minimum term of 235 years in prison.

Summary:

From 1950 to 2000, you can see an obvious trend among the mass murders - nearly all of them involved firearms, and nearly all of them were the result of some kind of psychological disturbance. In the next chapter, we'll examine mass murders that occurred between 2000 and present day.

CHAPTER 3
2000 through 2017

———————◆———————

As you read through this next chapter, you may notice a steep increase in the the death tolls for many of these events, along with an increase in frequency for these events, and an increase in the use of firearms.

TIMELINE

2000 - Wakefield Massacre
2001 - Isla Vista Murders
2001 - Nevada County Shootings
2001 - Greyhound Bus Attack]
2001 - Twin Towers
2003 - Lockhead Martin Shooting
2004 - Deltona Massacre
2005 - Red Lake Indian Reservation
2005 - Glendale Train Crash
2006 - Goleta Post Office
2006 - Amish School Shooting
2007 - Trolley Square Shooting
2007 - Virginia Tech School Shooting
2007 - Westroads Mall Shooting
2008 - Northern Illinois Univ. Shooting
2009 - Farmville Murders
2009 - Carthage Nursing Home

2009 - American Civic Assoc. Shooting

2009 - Fort Hood Shootings

2010 - University of Alabama Shooting

2010 - Hartford Distributors Shooting

2011 - Seal Beach Shooting

2011 - Maksim Gelman Murders

2011 - Tucson Shootings

2012 - Century 16 Theater Shooting

2012 - Wisconsin Sikh Temple Shooting

2012 - Sandy Hook Elementary School

2013 - Navy Yard Shooting

2013 - Santa Monica Shooting

2013 - West Fertilizer Co. Explosion

2014 - Isla Vista Stabbing/Shooting

2014 - Fort Hood Shooting

2015 - Charleston Church Massacre

2015 - Chattanooga Shooting

2015 - Umpqua Community College

2015 - Planned Parenthood Shooting

2015 - Inland Regional Center Shooting

2016 - Pulse Nightclub Shooting

2017 - First Baptist Church Shooting

2017 - Las Vegas Massacre

2018 - Stoneman Douglas High School

2000 - Wakefield Massacre - Wakefield, Massachusetts

On December 26th, Michael McDermott shot and killed seven coworkers at the Edgewater Technology plant where he worked. Investigators found that McDermott's wages had been garnished by the IRS as a result of child support taxes he had failed to pay.

They believe this garnishment was the reason for the shooting spree. When McDermott was apprehended, he told police that he had "been born without a soul," and that "God had allowed him to earn his soul by travelling through time to kill Hitler and six other Nazis." He was ultimately found guilty and sentenced to seven consecutive life terms, without possibility of parole.

2001 - Isla Vista Killings - California

On February 23rd, David Attias drove his vehicle at 65 miles per hour down Sabado Tarde Road, hitting five pedestrians. Four of those pedestrians died at the scene, and the fifth died many years later as a result of the injuries sustained. After hitting the pedestrians, Attias stopped the car, got out of the vehicle and began shouting that he was the "Angel of Death." He was then apprehended by a California Highway Patrol officer. Attias was ultimately found guilty but legally insane. He was sentenced to spend sixty years in Patton State Hospital mental institution. In 2012, Attias was granted conditional release on the assertion that his bipolar disorder was under control. He is now taking part in a supervised "but unlocked" outpatient treatment program.

2001 - Nevada County Shootings - California

On January 10th, Scott Thorpe killed three people and wounded two others in two different altercations in Nevada County, California. The first event occurred in the Nevada County Department of

Behavioral Health, where Thorpe opened fire at the reception desk. Thorpe fled the scene moments later, drove three miles away, and stopped at Lyon's Restaurant, where he shot the manager and restaurant cook. Thorpe fled the scene of that event, as well, and returned home. Once at home, he called his brother, a Sacramento County Sheriff's Deputy, and confessed to the shootings. Nevada County authorities were notified, and after a three-hour standoff, Thorpe was apprehended.

During the investigation, Thorpe explained that he went to the Behavioral Health Department because he was unhappy with the level and quality of care he had been receiving there. He went on to explain that he chose Lyon's Restaurant, because he believed the employees there had tried to poison him. Given his long and well-documented history of mental unrest and disturbance, Thorpe was quickly deemed incompetent to stand trial, and he was found not guilty by reason of insanity. Today, he is held in Napa State Hospital mental institution for continued treatment.

2001 - Greyhound Bus Attack - Manchester, Tennessee

On October 3rd, Damir Igric hijacked a Greyhound bus after attempting to kill the driver by slashing his throat with a knife. During the tussle with the bus driver, the bus crashed, and seven other people died - including Igric. Twenty-one passengers sought treatment for injuries sustained in the crash, but miraculously, the bus driver survived. Igric was in the United States on an expired visa from Croatia. His motives for the attack remain unknown, but he investigators were able to establish a long history of mental illness.

2001 - Twin Towers or 9/11 - New York City

On the morning of September 11th, four coordinated and simultaneous terrorist attacks occurred in the northeast United States. A total of 2,996 people were killed, and over 6,000 people were injured. In addition, approximately $10 billion dollars in damage occurred. This has been, by far, the largest act of mass murder in the history of the United States.

Each attack was carried out with an airplane. Nineteen different al-Qaeda terrorists hijacked four different passenger planes. Two of the flights were diverted and made to crash into each of the Twin Towers of the World Trade Center. Less than two hours after the impact, each of the 110-story towers collapsed.

The third passenger plane was diverted to the Pentagon, where it crashed into the building and caused the west side of the structure to collapse. The fourth and final plane was diverted toward Washington D.C., with the intention of crashing the plane into the White House. Passengers on the fourth plane were able to prevent that, and instead, the fourth plane crashed into an empty field in Stonycreek Township, Pennsylvania.

In addition to those that died on impact in each crash, over four hundred first responders (firefighters, paramedics, and law enforcement) were also killed in the aftermath.

al-Qaeda was immediately suspected for the attack, although they did not officially claim responsibility for it until three years later. As a result of the attack, the United States began the War on Terror, which was primarily focused on the destruction of al-Qaeda and the military invasion of both Iraq and Afghanistan.

2003 - Lockhead Martin Shooting - Meridian, Mississippi

On July 8th, Douglas Williams shot fourteen of his coworkers, killing six of them, at the Lockhead Martin plant where he was employed. That day, Williams stormed out of a mandatory ethics meeting and returned with several guns. He opened fire on his coworkers. After several minutes of indiscriminate shooting, Williams then made his way through the plant in search of a colleague that had previously reported him to management for making racist threats. He shot several more colleagues during his search and did not stop shooting until he came upon his girlfriend, Shirley, who also worked at the plant. As she was pleading with him to stop, Williams shot himself in the chest. No official motive was ever determined, but many people believe that Williams was motivated by racial issues, depression, and a general feeling of being misunderstood and mistreated by coworkers and management.

2004 - Deltona Massacre or Xbox Murders - Deltona, Florida

On August 6th, four men broke into a home in Deltona, Florida, and bludgeoned six people to death, as well as a dog. The motive behind the attack was retaliation against one of the victims. The attackers believed she was responsible for the eviction of one of the attackers, and that she had stolen property (including an Xbox game system) that he had left behind in the home she was now renting. All four attackers (Troy Victorino, Jerone Hunter, Robert Cannon and Michael Salas) were found guilty. Cannon and Salas were sentenced to life in prison. Meanwhile, Victorino and Hunter were originally sentenced to death, but those sentences have since been overturned.

2005 - Red Lake Indian Reservation - Red Lake, Minnesota

On March 21st, Jeffrey Weise killed his grandfather, who happened to be a tribal police officer, and his grandfather's girlfriend in their home. He then stole a number of his grandfather's police weapons, as well as a bulletproof vest, and drove to Red Lake Senior High School (from which he had graduated the year before). After entering the school, Weise shot and killed seven people, including a security guard and a teacher, and wounded five others. When police arrived, they exchanged gunfire with Weise, wounding him. Weise then committed suicide in an empty classroom.

Weise had a difficult upbringing, with his father committing suicide when Weise was eight, and his mother suffered severe brain damage after a car accident when Weise was ten. Weise was also bullied in school by classmates, and often expressed frustration about living in Red Lake.

2005 - Glendale Train Crash - Los Angeles, California
On January 26th, a commuter train collided with an SUV that had been abandoned on the train tracks. After hitting the SUV, the train jackknifed and struck two other trains - one stationary freight train and another commuter train traveling in the opposite direction. The collisions resulted in eleven deaths. The owner of the SUV, Juan Alvarez, was arrested and charged with eleven counts of murder. Alvarez claimed he had parked his car on the tracks with the intention of committing suicide, but he panicked at the last minute and abandoned the car. Alvarez was sentenced to eleven consecutive life sentences.

2006 - Goleta Post Office - Goleta, California
On January 30th, Jennifer San Marco first shot and killed her neighbor, then drove to the Goleta postal processing plant where she once worked and opened fire, killing six coworkers before committing suicide.

Investigators later determined that San Marco had a history of paranoia and mental illness, and that she may have believed she was the target of a conspiracy that involved the Goleta post office - despite the fact that she no longer lived or worked in Goleta.

2006 - Amish School Shooting - Nickel Mines, Pennsylvania

On October 2nd, Charles Roberts took ten girls hostage in a one-room schoolhouse in the Old Order Amish community known as Nickel Mines. Roberts killed five of the ten girls and wounded three others. He then committed suicide inside the schoolhouse. Roberts' motive for the attack remains uncertain - in four separate suicide notes, Roberts discussed the death of newborn daughter twenty years prior, his general anger and frustration with God, and dreams he had been having that he thought were encouraging him to molest young girls. His true motive may never be known.

2007 - Trolley Square Shooting - Salt Lake City, Utah

On February 12th, Sulejman Talovic shot and killed five people, wounded four others, and was then shot dead by Salt Lake City Police. Talovic was a native of Bosnia, who immigrated to the United States ten years prior. He lived here legally, and had only a short juvenile record of what police described as "minor mischief." No motive was ever discovered, and the FBI did not believe the incident to be an act of terrorism - however, many media outlets chose to imply that

Talovic had a religious motive and that he was attempting to further the cause of radical Islam.

2007 - Virginia Tech Shooting - Blacksburg, Virginia

On April 16th, Seung-Hui Cho shot and killed thirty-two people, and wounded seventeen others, on the Virginia Tech school campus. Cho was an undergraduate student at the university at the time of the shooting. He committed suicide before he could be apprehended by police, several hours after the shooting occurred.

Cho was a South Korean citizen, studying in the United States on a student's visa. Cho had been diagnosed with severe anxiety disorder while in high school and spent many years in therapy and special education courses. Shortly after starting at Virginia Tech, Cho was accused of stalking two female classmates. As a result of the stalking case, a Virginia special justice found Cho to be mentally ill and ordered him to seek outpatient treatment. Because he was not institutionalized, and was only asked to seek outpatient treatment, Cho was still able to legally purchase a gun.

Investigators discovered that Cho had a history of psychological issues, and that he had been diagnosed with severe depression, anxiety disorders, and selective mutism. Many family members believed that Cho was actually autistic.

Investigators also found that Cho was often bullied for his issues with speech, as well as his race. Despite his well-documented history of issues throughout middle school and high school, Virginia Tech was not warned about Cho's issues, as privacy laws at the time would have prohibited his high school counselors and teachers from sharing that information with the university.

2007 - Westroads Mall Shooting - Omaha, Nebraska
On December 5th, Robert Hawkins entered a Von Maur department store in the Westroads Mall of Omaha, Nebraska, and opened fire. He killed eight people, wounded four, and then committed suicide.

An hour before the attack, Hawkins' mother contacted the Sheriff's Department and provided them with a suicide note Hawkins had left behind. Meanwhile, Hawkins used a semi-automatic rifle that he had stolen from his stepfather to attack shoppers inside the mall. The entire attack lasted approximately fifteen minutes, with police responding to the mall within five minutes.

Investigators found that Hawkins had a history of mental disturbance - and was even hospitalized for depression at age six. He spent four months in a mental health institution at age fourteen, for making homicidal threats towards his stepmother. He was hospitalized in psychiatric institutions on two separate occasions, and had been diagnosed with attention deficit disorder, oppositional defiant disorder, and a mood disorder. He was later expelled from high school but managed to obtain his GED. In the weeks prior to the shooting, he had been fired from his job for petty theft and had separated with his girlfriend. To make matters worse, Hawkins had attempted to enlist in the U.S. Army, but his enlistment was denied.

Shortly after the attack, Hawkins' suicide note was released in the media. In the three-page note, Hawkins expressed an interest in becoming famous for his actions and wanting to "go out in style."

2008 - Northern Illinois University Shooting - DeKalb, Illinois

On February 14th, Steven Kazmierczak opened fire on a crowd of university students in a classroom, killing five and injuring seventeen. He then committed suicide. Kazmierczak was a graduate student of the University of Illinois and had previously attended Northern Illinois University. Kazmierczak was known as a good student, but his girlfriend at the time of the shooting told police that he had stopped taking several prescription medications - including Xanax, Ambien, and Prozac - in the weeks leading up to the incident. Today, little is known or understood about his motives, and nearly everyone who knew him was genuinely surprised by his actions.

2009 - Farmville Murders - Farmville, Virginia

In September, Richard McCroskey murdered his girlfriend, Emma, her parents, and her friend, Melanie. All four people were bludgeoned to death with a hammer while they were sleeping. Authorities believe McCroskey was motivated by his failing relationship with Emma, and that he feared she would break up with him. McCroskey fled the scene of the murders, and while on the run, he made a call to police to confess to the murders. McCroskey was apprehended at the Richmond International Airport, where police found him sleeping in the baggage claim area. McCroskey was ultimately convicted and sentenced to life in prison.

2009 - Carthage Nursing Home Shooting - Carthage, North Carolina

On March 29th, Robert Stewart entered the Carthage Nursing Home in search of his estranged wife, who worked at the facility. While looking for her, he shot and killed eight people, and wounded a ninth. Stewart was confronted by a responding police officer in the hallway of the nursing home. When he refused to drop his weapon and fired a shot at the officer, the officer responded and shot Stewart in the chest. Stewart survived the gunshot wound and was ultimately sentenced to 179 years in prison - despite arguments made by his lawyer that he had been under the influence of Ambien at the time of the shooting.

2009 - American Civic Association Shooting - Binghamton, New York

On April 3rd, Jiverly Wong entered the American Civic Association immigration center in Binghamton, New York, and opened fire. Wong shot and killed fourteen people, and wounded four others, before killing himself. Wong was a naturalized American citizen, originally from Vietnam, who had attended English language classes at the immigration center. Wong's motive was unclear, despite a two-page handwritten letter that was sent to a local news station on the day of the attack. Much of the letter described Wong's paranoia, and his belief that law enforcement agents had been "secretly" visiting his residence, and that there was a conspiracy against him. Given Wong's poor grasp of the English language, much of his letter was unintelligible.

2009 - Fort Hood - Killeen, Texas

On November 5th, Nidal Hasan shot and killed thirteen people and wounded thirty others. Hasan was an U.S. Army Major, as well as a psychiatrist, stationed on the Fort Hood army base. Prior to the attack, Hasan had been in contact with a known terrorist from Yemen, and Hasan's online activity was being closely monitored by a joint terrorism task force. Hasan had also been preparing to deploy to Afghanistan with his unit. According to eyewitnesses, Hasan appeared to target soldiers during his rampage, and spared many civilians that crossed his path. Ultimately, Hasan was wounded during the gun battle, and the wound effectively paralyzed him. He was court-martialed on thirteen counts of premeditated murder and thirty-two counts of attempted murder and found guilty. Hasan was sentenced to death and remains on death row today.

2010 - University of Alabama - Huntsville, Alabama

On February 12th, Amy Bishop opened fire during a routine meeting of the biology department colleagues at the University of Alabama. Bishop, a professor, shot and killed three people and wounded three others. Approximately forty minutes into the staff meeting, Bishop stood up suddenly, took out a gun, and started shooting. Bishop's gun either jammed or she ran out of ammunition after several rounds, and her confusion over the jammed gun gave the victims the opportunity to push her out of the room and lock the door behind her. Bishop was immediately apprehended as she exited the building.

Investigators believe her motive was related a request for tenure that was denied by the university. Bishop initially responded to the denial by making accusations of sex discrimination. Upon further investigation, it was revealed that Bishop had a violent past, and that she had actually shot and killed her own brother many years prior, in what was ruled as an accident. She also had a reputation as a poor and unpopular teacher.

Bishop's lawyer argued in court that Bishop suffered from paranoid schizophrenia. During the trial, Bishop attempted suicide but survived. She pleaded not guilty by reason of insanity but was ultimately convicted and sentenced to life in prison.

2010 - Hartford Distributors Shooting - Manchester, Connecticut

On August 3rd, Omar Thornton was asked to resign from his position at Hartford Distributors, after video surveillance was found of Thornton stealing beer from the warehouse. After signing his resignation and being escorted out of the building, Thornton pulled to guns out of his lunch box and returned to the building. He opened fire and quickly killed eight coworkers and injured two others. Thornton hid in a locked office prior to committing suicide. He told a 911 operator that his motive was race-related discrimination in the workplace.

2011 - Seal Beach Shooting - Seal Beach, California

On October 12th, Scott Dekraai shot and killed eight people at a hair salon in Seal Beach and wounded another. Dekraai had been involved in a custody dispute with his ex-wife, who was an employee of the salon. After the shooting, Dekraai fled and was eventually apprehended about a mile away from the salon. Dekraai had previously been diagnosed with PTSD. He was ultimately found guilty and sentenced to eight consecutive life terms plus seven years.

2011 - Maksim Gelman - New York City

On February 11th, Maksim Gelman killed four people and wounded five others in a stabbing spree.

He first stabbed his stepfather fifty-five times, then killed the mother of a friend while waiting for the friend to return home. When the friend finally returned, Gelman stabbed her eleven times, and then fled the scene in his stepfather's car. After crashing the car into another car, Gelman stabbed the driver of that car and stole the vehicle. While fleeing, he also hit a pedestrian with the stolen car, killing him on impact. After abandoning the stolen car, Gelman flagged down a cab and stabbed the cab driver. He then approached yet another vehicle, and stabbed that driver, as well. After purchasing a ticket to board a train at Penn Station, Gelman also stabbed the ticket seller - then promptly boarded the train. At this point, over twenty-four hours had passed. A passenger on the train recognized Gelman from news coverage of the stabbing of his stepfather and notified police. Gelman was apprehended and disarmed on the train. Gelman pleaded guilty to all charges and was sentenced to two hundred years in prison. No specific motive was ever uncovered, but Gelman had a history of petty crime, drug use and drug dealing, and paranoid or antisocial tendencies.

2011 - Tucson Shooting - Tucson, Arizona

On January 8th, Jared Loughner opened fire at a political event, shooting eighteen people and killing six. He began the massacre by shooting Congressional Representative Gabrielle Giffords point-blank in the head, then firing on the crowd. Loughner was arrested at the scene, refused to cooperate with investigators, was eventually found incompetent to stand trial, as he had been diagnosed as a paranoid schizophrenic. In August of 2012, he was finally deemed competent, and he was sentenced to life in prison.

2012 - Century 16 Theater Shooting - Aurora, Colorado

On July 20th, during a midnight showing of the film *Dark Knight Rises*, James Holmes entered the theater, set off tear gas grenades, and opened fire on the audience. A total of twelve people were killed, and seventy others were injured. Fifty-eight of the injuries were related to the gunfire, while four injuries were tear gas related and eight other injuries were caused in the chaos as people tried to flee the theater.

Holmes was apprehended at the theater, in the parking lot beside his car. He was taken into custody without incident. He confessed to the massacre but chose to plea "not guilty by reason of insanity." Holmes made several suicide attempts while awaiting his trial but was ultimately tried and found guilty. He was sentenced to twelve life sentences and an additional 3,318 additional years.

2012 - Wisconsin Sikh Temple Shooting - Oak Creek, Wisconsin

On August 5th, Wade Page shot and killed six people, and wounded four others, before committing suicide. Page was an Army veteran and known White

Supremacist. It is assumed that he was racially motivated in the attack.

2012 - Sandy Hook Elementary School - Newton, Connecticut

On December 14th, Adam Lanza killed his mother while she slept, stole her rifle, then drove to Sandy Hook Elementary, where he opened fire - killing twenty children and six adults. Lanza committed suicide when police arrived. The entire incident, from start to suicide, lasted five minutes.

Lanza's motive for the shooting is unknown, although the investigation implied that Lanza may have had Asperger's syndrome, as well as anxiety, depression, and obsessive-compulsive disorder. Reports also suggested that he may have had an unusual preoccupation with death and violence.

2013 - Navy Yard Shooting - Washington D.C.

On September 16th, Aaron Alexis shot and killed twelve people, and injured three others at the Washington Navy Yard. While hiding in a bank of cubicles, officers successfully shot and killed Alexis.

During the investigation, FBI agents found notes on Alexis' computer that implied Alexis believed he was the victim of harassment, that he heard voices in his head, and that "someone was trying to control [him] with low frequency electromagnetic waves."

2013 - Santa Monica Shooting - Santa Monica, California

On June 7th, John Zawahri shot and killed six people, and injured another four. The attack took place near a college campus and was related to a domestic dispute. Prior to the shooting, Zawahri had shot two men in his homes and then set the house on fire. When police arrived at the scene of the shooting, Zawahri opened fire on police and was subsequently killed by police.

2013 - West Fertilizer Company Explosion - West, Texas

On April 17th, fifteen people were killed and 160 were injured in an explosion at the West Fertilizer Company in West, Texas. The incident began when a fire was deliberately set inside the facility. When the facility reached two large ammonia tanks and a large stash of ammonium nitrate fertilizer stored at the facility, the tanks and fertilizer exploded. It is still unknown who set the fire, or why the fire was set.

2014 - Isla Vista, California

On May 23rd, Elliot Rodgers killed six people and injured fourteen others in an attack near the University of California Santa Barbara campus. Rodgers started by stabbing three men at this apartment, then he traveled to a sorority house near campus and shot three female students. He continued driving and wound up a local deli, where he shot another male student. He then proceeded to speed through the Isla Vista neighborhood, shooting at pedestrians indiscriminately. He ultimately wound up exchanging gunfire with police, and the chase did not end until Rodgers crashed his car into a parked vehicle and immediately committed suicide. During the investigation, officers found that Rodgers had uploaded a video to YouTube shortly before the attack, in which he stated that he wanted to "punish women for rejecting [him]," as well as punish "men who were sexually active," as he envied them. Investigators also found that while Rodgers had never been officially diagnosed with a mental disorder, a psychiatrist had prescribed him an antipsychotic medication, most often used to treat schizophrenia and bipolar disorder, and that Rodgers had refused to take the medication as prescribed. Rodgers mother also claimed he had been diagnosed with Asperger syndrome - although that claim could not be proven.

2014 - Fort Hood, Texas

On April 2nd, Ivan Lopez shot and killed three people, wounded fourteen, and then committed suicide. Lopez was an Army Specialist, and shortly before the attack, he had requested a ten-day leave so that he could attend to a family issue. When his leave request was denied, Lopez became upset. He returned to the same building where he had requested leave and opened fire. At the time of the massacre, Lopez was being treated for PTSD, depression and anxiety. He also believed that other soldiers in his unit were bullying him, and he had requested a transfer to a different unit.

2015 - Charleston Church Massacre - Charleston, South Carolina

On June 17th, Dylan Roof entered a church during a prayer service and opened fire on the African American church members, killing nine of them and injuring three others. Roof attempted to commit suicide in order to evade police capture but had run out of ammunition. He was subsequently apprehended, found guilty on all charges, and sentenced to death. Upon investigation, it became clear that Roof was a proud White Supremacist.

2015 - Chattanooga, Tennessee

On July 16th, Muhammad Abdulazeez opened fire on a military recruiting center and a U.S. Navy Reserve center in Chattanooga, Tennessee. He killed five and injured two, before being killed by police. Abdulazeez was a naturalized American citizen, from Kuwait, who had migrated to the United States in 1996. Investigators found that Abdulazeez had a history of drug and alcohol abuse, and that he may have been abusing sleeping pill, opioids and marijuana in the weeks before the massacre. In addition, Abdulazeez had recently filed for bankruptcy, and had been trying to seek treatment for depression.

2015 - Umpqua Community College - Roseburg, Oregon

On October 1st, Chris Harper-Mercer shot and killed nine people and injured eight others in an attack at the community college where he was enrolled. Harper-Mercer committed suicide after engaging in gunfire with police. The investigation found that Harper-Mercer felt isolated, had White Supremacist tendencies, and that he was upset by his inability to have a successful sexual relationship with a woman. In addition, Harper-Mercer had been suspended from the community college in the weeks prior to the attack, due to unpaid tuition.

2015 - Planned Parenthood Shooting - Colorado Springs, Colorado

On November 27th, Robert Dear, Jr., shot and killed three people, and injured nine, during a shooting inside a Planned Parenthood office in Colorado Springs. Dear's motive for the shooting centered on his pro-life views, and in interviews with police, he referred to himself as a "warrior for babies." Dear was ultimately found incompetent to stand trial and has been confined to a Colorado state mental institution.

2015 - Inland Regional Center - San Bernardino, California

On December 2nd, Syed Farook and Tashfeen Malik, a married couple, shot and killed fourteen people, and wounded twenty-two others in an attack at the Inland Regional Center of the San Bernardino

County Department of Public Health. They fled the scene and were pursued by police and were ultimately shot and killed by police four hours after the initial incident.

Farook was a U.S.-born citizen, and Malik was a lawful U.S. resident, although he was born in Pakistan. Upon investigation, the FBI found that the couple were "homegrown violent extremists" and that they were not a part of any known terrorist cell or network, but that they had expressed an extreme commitment to jihadism.

2016 - Pulse Nightclub - Orlando, Florida
On June 12th, Omar Mateen shot and killed forty-nine and wounded fifty-three others in an attack on a gay nightclub in Orlando. The attack led to a three-hour standoff with police, which ended when police shot and killed Mateen.

During the attack, Mateen told a 911 operator that he swore allegiance to the Islamic State of Iraq and blamed the death of Abu Waheeb for his decision to commit mass murder. Mateen's attack is the deadliest LGBT incident in U.S. history, although reports suggest that Mateen had no idea the club catered to members of the LGBT community.

2017 - First Baptist Church Shooting - Sutherland Springs, Texas

On November 5th, Devin Kelley entered a Baptist church in Sutherland Springs during the regular Sunday morning service and opened fire on the worshipers. Kelley killed twenty-six and injured another twenty. As he exited the church, he was confronted by a former NRA firearms instructor, who was also armed. The instructor, Stephen Willeford, shot Kelley twice - once in the torso and once in the leg. Kelley fired back, but missed, got into his car, and fled the scene.

As Kelley fled, Willeford flagged down a passing truck, got in, and convinced the driver to follow Kelley. During the high-speed pursuit, the driver of the pick-up truck called 911 to report their location, so that a few police units would be dispatched in their direction. Kelley ultimately lost control of his vehicle and crashed in a field. When police got to the car, they found Kelley dead - with a third gunshot wound to the head, which was self-inflicted.

During the investigation, officers found that Kelley had targeted that specific church because his estranged wife occasionally attended church services there. While his wife not at the church during the attack, her grandmother was and her grandmother died at the scene. Kelley had a history of disciplinary issues and violent behavior. He was even dishonorably discharged from the army after he assaulted his first wife and step-son.

2017 - Las Vegas

On October 1st, Stephen Paddock opened fire on a crowd at a music festival in Las Vegas, firing his weapons from a hotel room on the 32nd floor of a building near the festival. Fifty-eight people were killed, 851 people were injured, and more than 1000 rounds of ammunition were fired. Approximately an hour after the shooting began, his body was found in his hotel room - it appeared he had died of a self-inflicted gunshot wound to the head.

This massacre remains the deadliest shooting in American history. Paddock used an arsenal of weapons - including AR-15s with bump stocks and large capacity magazines, AR-10 rifles, and more. The total count of compiled weapons found in his hotel room came to twenty-four guns.

Police response was much longer than it should have been, as Paddock was firing these weapons from 2,000 feet away and it was difficult to tell where the shots were coming from and how many shooters were involved. Ultimately, police were clued into Paddock's location by the windows of his hotel room - which had been shattered.

Despite an intense investigation, Paddock's motive remains unknown. Some theorize that he was upset about money lost while gambling, others theorized that he may have had an accomplice. At one point, members of ISIS claimed responsibility and claimed that Paddock was one of their soldiers - but no proof of a connection to ISIS has ever been found.

2018 - Stoneman Douglas High School Shooting - Parkland, Florida

On February 14th, Nikolas Cruz entered his former high school and opened fire, killing fourteen students and three staff members, and wounding seventeen others. That afternoon, Cruz arrived at the school shortly before the dismissal bell rang. Upon entering the building, Cruz set off the fire alarm, and then stood in hallway, firing his weapons indiscriminately as people followed the fire alarm procedures of evacuation. After approximately six minutes of shooting, Cruz calmly walked away - blending in with the fleeing students. He walked to a nearby Walmart, where he purchased a soda, and approximately an hour later, he was arrested without incident while walking through a suburban neighborhood.

Cruz had been expelled from the school the year prior and was attending a GED program at the time of the shooting. Cruz had a history of behavioral issues and making threats against other students. At one point, Stoneman Douglas had actually banned him from carrying a backpack on campus, due to the gravity of the threats he made against other students. A YouTube channel belonging to Cruz was flagged for violent videos in 2016, but the videos could never be officially traced back to Cruz. In addition, an anonymous call was made in January of 2018 to the FBI, warning that Cruz was planning a school shooting. That anonymous was never reported to the local FBI office, and it as never investigated.

Investigators found a number of posts, written by Cruz, on social media that suggested he had racist, anti-Semitic, homophobic and anti-immigrant views. Several pieces of evidence were collected at the scene and found to have swastikas carved into them. In the ten years leading up to the shooting, Parkland's police department received twenty-three different complaints about Cruz and his behavior. When interviewing the surviving students, many said that they were not surprised that Cruz did it.

Ultimately, Cruz as charged with seventeen counts of first-degree murder and seventeen counts of attempted murder. He refused to enter a plea, so a "not guilty" plea was entered for him. Cruz is currently awaiting trial, pending further mental health evaluations.

Summary:
As you can see from the information provided in his chapter, mass murders are not only becoming more frequently, but more people are dying, as well. This is, in large part, due to lax gun laws - as nearly every mass murder from 1950 to today was carried out with firearms. In addition, you may have noticed that mental health continues to be a prevalent theme - with

nearly every perpetrator suffering from some sort of mental disturbance.

In the next chapter, we will discuss one of the two most common motives for mass murder: ideology. Ideology refers to personal believes, political beliefs, and religion. The other most common motive for mass murder is mental health, which we will discuss in the fifth chapter.

CHAPTER 4

The Ideology of a Mass Murderer

———————●———————

As you may have noticed while reading through the three previous chapters, mass murders are becoming more and more frequent. It would be fair to say that we have come to expect a mass shooting of some kind on a monthly basis - and that we are no longer surprised when these shootings occur in schools or workplaces. The routine has become commonplace and depressingly familiar - especially as so many of these events are the result of "copycat killers" or people who crave the spotlight.

A hundred years ago, the only reports of mass murders came through print newspapers. This meant a limited audience, as newspaper circulation was not widespread, and many Americans could not afford to buy a newspaper (and some would have been unable to read that newspaper). As journalism has changed, and as technology has overwhelmed us, we have found ours stuck in a twenty-four-hour news cycle, where news organizations feel obligated to talk about the same events, repeatedly, for hours at a time. This kind of news coverage leads to a certain level of fame or notoriety, which can be reason enough for a mass murderer to kill dozens of people. They all tend to believe that five minutes of fame is better than being forgotten - no matter what that fame is for.

So, what motivates one person to kill others - especially many others? Is it religion, race, or some other bias? Are violent video games, movies and music to blame? Do these murders come from broken homes? Are they bullied? Do they have low IQs? Are they mentally ill?

The answers to all of these questions is a simply yes. All of those reasons are reasons that have been given to justify the actions of mass murderers.

A forensic psychiatrist named James Knoll has studied these questions extensively. He cites a 2013 Congressional Research Service report that first defines mass murder as "an event that occurs in a relatively public place and involves four or more deaths." This report identified seventy-eight public mass shooting between 1983 and 2013 - which resulted in a total of 547 deaths and 1,023 injuries.

Knoll also points out that nearly all of the perpetrators are young males, and that they typically act alone before and during the event. Most of these young men have a history of odd behavior and a strange fascination with weapons.

Knoll goes on to explain that there are several "common psychological themes" present in most of his case studies - nearly every mass murderer displays feelings of resentment to both real and imagined injustices and rejections. Nearly every mass murderer becomes hyper-focused on feelings of humiliation. They typically suffer from chronic and overwhelming feelings of envy, paranoia, social persecution, and jealousy. These mass murderers typically feel like they have no power, and no control over their life. They become aggravated and start to feel entitled to a certain kind of life. Unable to obtain that certain kind of life, they decide to take matters into their own hands.

Mass murderers typically take a violent path because violence inherently provides a sense of power, even if it is only a sense of pseudo-power. Violent acts give the opportunity to take retribution for the way they have been made to feel and allows them to destroy other people just as they feel others have attempted to destroy them. Mass murderers typically feel a deep sense of despair, fury and outright selfishness - and they use they feelings to justify their actions. They also typically expect not to survive what they are planning, and they almost always commit suicide after committing their violent acts. The vast majorities of mass murders can be classified as murder-suicides.

While mental illness and mental disorders absolutely play a large role in the "making of" a mass murderer, there is a lot of debate about the effect an environment can have on a person, and whether the "tipping point" for a mass murderer is their mental health or their environment. By environment, we are referring to political, moral, or religious grounds that could be exacerbated or lead to extremist tendencies.

Much of the argument boils down to nature versus nurture - are mass murderers more likely to commit murder if they grow up in a broken home, in a devout religion, or in an isolated community? Or are they more likely to commit murder because of a simple predisposition to mental illness? There is no right answer to these questions, and in most case studies, a degree of truth was found on both sides of the argument.

Think back over the mass murders we outlined in previous chapters. Many of them had religious, moral, or racial motives. The motive behind the Planned Parenthood shooting was a combination of religion and morality - as the perpetrator was a firm believer in the pro-life movement. He believed that those that worked for Planned Parenthood and those that took advantage of their wide array of medical services were immoral, corrupt, and living a life of sin. He believed that by killing them, he was protecting unborn babies.

The motive behind the Charleston Church massacre was racial - the perpetrator was a known White Supremacist, and he deliberately chose a church that was known to have a predominately African American congregation.

Each time a mass murderer is deemed "incompetent to stand trial," or is successful in their plea of "not guilty by reason of insanity," there is an outcry from the public and the family of the victims to change legislation relating to mental health. Many people disagree with the assertion that moral disagreements can amount to mental illness, and even more people disagree with the way the mentally ill are persecuted and punished.

Culture, politics, spirituality and religion create the framework for which we understand and view the world. This framework has a profound effect on the way we live our lives, and for some people, this framework provides the necessary justification for extreme actions.

Some psychiatrists have attempted to put together a practical guide to help identify when religious beliefs reach a point of "psychiatric morbidity," or extremism. This guideline states that:

- There must be recognizable symptoms of mental illness in multiple areas of the patient's life - such delusions, mood disturbances, hallucinations, thought disorders and more.
- The experience (or crime) must be self-described as containing a symptom of

psychiatric illness - i.e. a delusion, or the assertion that the patient "blacked out."

● The lifestyle and behavior of the patient must follow a path that is consistent with the progression of mental illness - i.e. it becomes difficult for the patient to hold down a job or maintain personal relationships.

● There must be evidence of a disordered personality in matters beyond the specific motive - i.e. if the patient claims his motive was based on religion, then disorder must be identified in another aspect of his life beyond religion.

● The preceding points must be identifiable in the patient's life prior to the attack or event - and not simply present on the day of or in the days proceeding. Especially when you consider that nearly all mental disorders and illnesses are the result of the patient's life circumstances,

These guidelines may become essential when trying to determine if someone is simply suffering from mental illness or if they are suffering from true psychopathy. And regardless of whether or not the perpetrator is suffering from true psychopathy or not - what is the appropriate method of treatment?

Are those who suffer from mental illness and commit heinous crimes as a result of their illness deserving of jail time or a death sentence? Or can they be rehabilitated in a state institution? Even psychologists have a hard time making that assessment. Some mental illnesses are easier to treat than others. Some patients are easier to treat than others. And even with the best treatment and most successful treatment, there is always the risk that the perpetrator will relapse or stop taking their psychiatric medications. Is that risk acceptable? Is it appropriate to ask the general public to accept a risk like that?

If a mass murder is committed for no reason other than the ideology of the perpetrator, and no mental illness or defect can be determined, the perpetrator is usually sentenced to life in prison or sentenced to death. But if the perpetrator is found "not guilty by reason of insanity," they are typically required to seek inpatient treatment at a state mental institution. Is that a just punishment, given the gravity of the crimes committed? Many people think not.

While it is fairly easy to identify people that may belong to a "high risk" group, it is nearly impossible to identify which people within that group are likely to "snap" or lose their grip on reality. There would virtually no way to track someone of a high-risk group without violating their civil rights. There are millions of devout, pro-life Christians in the world - we cannot add them all to a "watch list" in anticipation of another Planned Parenthood shooting. That would not only be unethical, but impossible.

So, if we cannot monitor citizens for their beliefs and ideologies, what can we do? We can monitor their mental health, provide greater mental health resources and education, and make a greater effort as a community to support our community members.

Always remember to take news coverage of mass murders with a large grain of salt. Media outlets tend to politicize and sensationalize these events. Many people assume that perpetrators of mass murders are usually foreigners or immigrants - in reality, they are usually white. Between 1982 and 2018, white perpetrators were responsible for 56 out of 97 mass shootings. 16 of those shootings had black perpetrators; there were seven each for Asians and Latinos, three for Native Americans, and the final eight were unknown or other.

In addition, many people tend to overlook the fact that mass murderers are predominantly male. Between 1982 and 2018, only 2 of 96 perpetrators were women. So, remember: these events are not always as they are portrayed. They are often politicized and sensationalized, with hundreds of conspiracy theories tacked onto them. Every story has two sides, and every action has a motive - unfortunately, some stories cannot be told, and some motives cannot be discovered when the perpetrator has chosen to die.

In the next chapter, we will discuss the psychology and psychological tendencies of mass murderers - along with what we can do to prevent mass murderers.

CHAPTER 5

The Psychology of a Mass Murderer

———◦———

When we discuss the psychology of a mass murderer, we first must acknowledge the trends that are easily recognizable. Nearly all mass murderers are young men, nearly all of them suffer from some degree of paranoia, depression, or anxiety. Nearly all of them feel powerless, for one reason or another, and they go to great lengths to regain the power they feel they lost - even to the point of committing mass murder.

Traditionally, from the point of view of a psychological profiler, men exist in a world bound by status. "Toxic masculinity" is a genuine issue, as many men are raised to adopt certain personality traits (like aggression), and if they fail to adopt those tendencies, they are ridiculed as weak or feminine. Toxic masculinity is even worse for men that struggle to make romantic connections with women. Nearly 60% of men do not reproduce, which provides an automatic sense of success to those who do reproduce. Reproduction is seen as a status symbol or honor - so those that are unable to procreate, whether the reason is physical or emotional, struggle with their sense and understanding of their own masculinity. Some men are successful in transferring that sense of frustration into other outlets - like sports or their career. Others are not, and they wind up expressing themselves in unhealthy or violent ways.

One study actually identified the causes of mass murder by archiving seventy different mass murder events. They found that mass murder was far more common if firearms were readily available to the perpetrator. These mass murders not only had a larger number of casualties but were usually methodically planned and paired with other methods, like bombs. Whereas, those that did not have easy access to firearms relied on methods like stabbing and fire - where there were fewer casualties and a lot less planning involved. In countries with strict gun laws, most mass murders are vehicular in nature - meaning that the perpetrator chose to deliberately drive or crash a vehicle into a crowd of people. Vehicular mass murder leads to a lot of damage, in a short amount of time, and usually garners an unhealthy level of attention or fame from news media outlets.

The same study looked at the common denominators among mass murderers and found that the average age was thirty-three years - although the ages ranged from as young as eleven to as old as sixty-six. They also found that the younger the perpetrator was, the more likely they had a history of petty theft or crime, and that they had several encounters with law enforcement prior to the major events. The younger perpetrators were also more likely to allow themselves to be apprehended by police, meaning they were less likely to commit suicide or try to force suicide by cop. In addition, the younger the perpetrator, the more likely investigators were to find a history of bullying, depression, and anxiety.

Meanwhile, the older the perpetrator, the more likely they were to be married or have families, and the less likely they were to have exhibited symptoms of mental illness or have signs of legal trouble. They were, however, more likely to have recently lost a "status symbol," like their job or custody of their children.

Beyond the "toxic masculinity" and the associated psychological issues with loss of status or power, the other primary reasons behind mass murders is simple mental health. In some cases, the cause is a severe mental health break - like schizophrenia or psychosis. In other cases, the cause is mental health issues that have become overwhelming - like depression, anxiety, or paranoia.

It is especially important to consider mental health when talking about young perpetrators. Nearly every mass murderer under the age of twenty-five was known to have suffered from a wealth of mental health issues. Many of them were autistic or considered to at least be on the autism spectrum. Many of them came from broken homes, struggled with social interactions at school, and suffered from either depression and/or anxiety. Worst of all - many of them had attempted to seek treatment for their issues, but the treatment was either subpar, they lacked the support system they needed to continue with treatment, or they were prescribed prescription medications that did little or nothing to help ease the conditions with which they suffered from.

In the United States, there is an undeniable mental health crisis. Many insurance policies do not cover counseling, or if they do, they cover a very limited number of counseling sessions each year. Insurance companies also limit and restrict the prescription medications available to the insured. This makes it incredibly difficult for parents to seek treatment for their children. and for those with low incomes to seek treatment for themselves.

To make matters worse - many schools are not equipped with properly trained counseling staff. More often than not, school counselors were shuffled into that position from another, and there is little (if any) training involved. They also have a very limited support network, and their hands are often tied by medical privacy laws when it comes to reporting potential threats.

If you consider the mass murderers that were under the age of twenty-one, it will become clear that each of those individuals could have benefited greatly from a highly-trained professional in the psychology field. A lot of the violence could have been avoided if they had received proper treatment and support.

Mental Health America, a community-based non-profit, released a study in 2017 that showed one in five adult Americans suffer from some sort of mental health condition - whether it is as "mild" as anxiety or as "severe" as schizophrenia. That amounts to more than forty million Americans and is more than the populations of Florida and New York combined.

They also found that the mental health of American youths is getting worse. Rates of severe depression in youths has increased to 8.2% from 5.9%. Worse yet, 76% of those suffering from severe depression receive no treatment or inadequate treatment.

Overall, access to treatment and insurance has improved, thanks to the Affordable Care Act - but many Americans still have trouble accessing that care. Nearly 55% of American adults that suffer from a mental illness do not receive any treatment at all. Since the Affordable Care Act passed, the rate of uninsured adults with a mental illness has decreased by 5%, and the states that increased their Medicaid expansion saw an increase in the number of American youths that sought and received mental health care and treatment for their mental health disorders.

Mental Health America also found that nearly half of Americans with a mental health condition also have a substance abuse disorder, and nearly ten million Americans experience suicidal ideation. In addition - there are not enough trained and qualified mental health workers in the United States. Studies shows that each mental healthcare worker has six times the patient load that is recommended for appropriate and adequate treatment. This includes every level of treatment: psychologists and psychiatrists, social workers, psychiatric nurses, and counselors. For example: In Alabama, there is only one trained and qualified mental health professional for every 1,260 residents.

Obviously, we should increase the funding available for mental health, encourage more people to enter the mental health workforce, and improve the accessibility of mental health care - but those actions simply are not enough. We must do more.

What else can we do to prevent mass murders? The first and most obvious step, given how frequently guns are used to perpetrate mass murder, is pass stricter gun laws in the United States. The theory behind this is simple: if it's harder to buy a gun, it will be harder to commit mass murder.

Many pro-gun advocates argue against this mindset, insisting that if someone does not have access to a gun, they will simply find another way - they will build a bomb, go on a stabbing spree, commit arson. Pro-gun advocates are known for insisting that "guns don't kill people; people kill people." This is not a false statement, but it is a naive statement. While it would be very difficult to kill dozens of people with a knife - it has happened. And while gunfire is the easiest way to kill a large number of people at one time, bombs are just as effective.

It does not help matters that most gun laws are decided on a state-by-state basis. Some states allow you to carry a concealed weapon without a permit, while others do not. Some states allow you to own a gun, but not register it, while others do not. some states allow you to own specific attachments for your weapons (like high capacity magazine, bump stocks, and more), while others do not. And scariest of all - a number of people have successfully created a functional (and deadly) gun using only a 3D printer. Private gun sales are also a major problem, as many states (like Arizona) have virtually no rules regarding private gun sales or "gifts."

Stricter gun laws (like requiring background checks or mental health evaluations) will lead to fewer shootings, but may not lead to fewer mass murders, guns are not always the "weapon of choice." So, what else can we do?

We can make therapy/counseling easier to obtain. It is currently easier (and cheaper) to purchase a gun than it is to obtain a year of counseling or therapy from a licensed professional. The mental health industry is grossly underfunded, and often inaccessible to those that need it most. If anything is going to change, reforming the mental health industry is something that must change.

It is absolutely fair to say that no mass murderer is truly healthy or of sound mind. They all suffer from some degree of mental illness, and they all felt as if they did not have the support they needed in their daily life. The best thing we can do, as a community, is provide support to those who need it most. The old adage "if you see something, say something," absolutely applies.

If you have a coworker or fellow student who seems isolated or quiet, reach out. Many people who wind up committing such heinous acts struggle to make connections with people, and to have healthy relationships. If we can step outside our own comfort zones and reach out to those that might need a little more assistance than others, we could prevent the next mass murder. If we can work together to stop or minimize bullying -- especially internet bullying, we could prevent the next mass murder. And if we are all more aware of the warning signs of mental illness and instability, we could prevent the next mass murder.

For more information about what you can do, and what resource are available not only to you but also to someone who may be "at risk," contact the National

Institute of Mental Health. You can visit them online at https://www.nimh.nih.gov/health/find-help/index.shtml.

For an immediate crisis - you can also call the National Suicide Prevention Hotline at 1-800-273-8255. The call is toll-free, and crisis counselors are available twenty-four hours a day, seven days a week.

If you need help finding a provider or mental health advocate, you can call the Substance Abuse and Mental Health Services Administration at 1-800-662-HELP (or 1-800-662-4357).

In addition, many states, counties and cities have mental health facilities that you may be able to contact. If you contact your local Health Department, they should be able to put in touch with the available resources. Universities and Community Colleges typically offer mental health or behavioral health services, as well.

As we discussed - the most important thing you can do is talk to someone, whether you are in crisis or you know someone who may be in crisis. It is not easy to ask for help when help is needed, and oftentimes, those in crisis believe that they are invisible and unimportant, and that the rest of the world does not understand and recognize the way they feel. Simply talking to a mental health professional has the potential to prevent a tragedy and save many, many lives.

Of course, if you witness strange or suspicious behavior, report it. Do not be afraid to call 911, and never assume that someone else has already notified law enforcement. It is better for the police to receive twenty calls about the same concern than none.

And finally - if you are a gun owner, and you choose to sell or get rid of your gun, consider selling it to a reputable gun store or gun broker or surrender it to your local police department. Purchasing a gun from retail store requires at least a minimal background check, whereas a private gun sale would not require a background check of any kind. You would not want your old gun to wind up in the hands of a murderer - so do what little you can to make sure it does not.

CONCLUSION

There are so many more mass murders than those detailed in this book. We made every effort to include not only the most famous events, but the most interesting events, as well. Mass murder has plagued the United States throughout its history, but in the last thirty years, these events have become more frequent, less predictable, and more violent.

Mass murder has traditionally been defined as any public event in which three or more people are murdered within a limited proximity to one another - with most events resulting in only four or five deaths. But in recent years, the rate of casualties due to mass murder has increased exponentially.

In fact - we are willing to bet that you, personally, cannot remember a single year in your life in which a mass murder did not make national news. From Columbine to 9/11 to Newton to Aurora to Las Vegas to Parkland - if you remember a time in your life when mass murder didn't exist… to be frank, you're wrong.

Without making major changes to gun legislation and the availability of mental health care and education, mass murders will only become more common, more violent and deadlier.

To be fair - even if guns did not exist, mass murder still would. As evidenced by several of the events detailed here in this book - mass murderers have used everything from knives to fire to bombs to hammers and other blunt instruments. However - without guns - death tolls and injury counts would certainly be lower.

As we stated before - many studies now show that public shootings are becoming more common in the United States, meanwhile the overall rate of firearm deaths has actually decreased by 50% since 1993. From 1982 to 2011, a mass shooting occurred nearly every two hundred days. From 2011 to 2014, a mass shooting has occurred every 64 days in the United States. Not all of those incidents have been classified as "mass murders," however, as many of them had few (if any) fatalities.

So, why are mass murders happening more often?

Some people point to the rather relaxed gun control laws in the United States, insisting that if gun laws were stronger, there would be fewer mass shootings. Some people point to an increase in mental health issues, insisting that if mental health was a greater priority, we would be able to prevent mass murders from happening. Others point to the media, insisting that if the media handled news coverage of mass murders differently, there may be fewer of them. Many people believe that there is a "copycat effect" or that many mass murderers are seeking fame and attention - therefore, news coverage should be limited in order to avoid sensationalizing the act.

Ultimately, there is no right answer. And ultimately, there is no way to know what the one, true problem is. We can blame gun laws, we can blame the media, we can blame the limitations of our mental health industry. But only changing one aspect will not solve the problem or ease the burden. We will have to work together, and we will have to work on fixing different angles. Restrictions on gun sales, minimizing sensationalist stories, and improving the quality of mental health care while also improving the accessibility of mental health care - these are the steps we need to take. We hope you agree, and we hope you will take the information we provided you with in this book to make the world a better, brighter, healthier place.

RESOURCES

- **<u>Anxiety and Depression Association of America (ADAA)</u>** provides information on prevention, treatment and symptoms of anxiety, depression and related conditions. Phone: 240-485-1001

- **<u>Children and Adults with Attention-Deficit/Hyperactivity Disorder (CHADD)</u>** provides information and referrals on ADHD, including local support groups. Phone: 800-233-4050

- **<u>Depression and Bipolar Support Alliance (DBSA)</u>** provides information on bipolar disorder and depression, offers in-person and online support groups and forums. Phone: 1-800-826-3632

- **<u>International OCD Foundation</u>** provides information on OCD and treatment referrals. Phone: 617-973-5801

- **<u>National Institute of Mental Health (NIMH)</u>** provides information on statistics, clinical trials and research. NAMI references NIMH statistics for our website and publications. Phone: 1-866-615-6464

- **<u>SAMHSA Treatment Locator</u>** provides referrals to low cost/sliding scale mental health care, substance abuse and dual diagnosis treatment. Phone: 800-662-4357

- **Schizophrenia and Related Disorders Alliance of America (SARDAA)**maintains the Schizophrenia Anonymous programs, which are self-help groups and are now available as toll free teleconferences. Phone: 240-423-9432

- **Sidran Institute** helps people understand, manage and treat trauma and dissociation; maintains a helpline for information and referrals. Phone: 410-825-8888

- **TARA (Treatment and Research Advancements for Borderline Personality Disorder)** offers a referral center for information, support, education and treatment options for BPD. Phone: 1-888-482-7227

- **The American Foundation for Suicide Prevention** provides referrals to support groups, mental health professionals, resources on loss and suicide prevention information. Phone: 1-888-333-2377

- **The National Domestic Violence Hotline** provides 24/7 crisis intervention, safety planning and information on domestic violence. Phone: 1-800-799-7233

- **The Suicide Prevention Lifeline** connects callers to trained crisis counselors 24/7. They also provide a chat function on their website. Phone: 1-800-273-8255

Thank you for making it through to the end of *Mass Murder: A Brief History of Mass Murder in America*. We hope that this book was not only informative, but that it helped provide you with a better understanding of why mass murders happen, and what can be done to stop them. There are many, many books on the subject available - and we are thrilled that you chose ours. Our goal was to provide you with a timeline of events, point out the common threads among each event, and help you to better understand why these things happen.

Please consider leaving an honest review of our book and thank you again for choosing our book.